Contents

Foreword..4

Introduction..6

Start Saving For A Down Payment Early........8

How Much House Can You Afford.............10

Understanding Your Credit.......................13

Stop Any New Credit Activity....................16

Explore Down Payment Options...............18

Research Assistance Programs..................20

Start Budgeting For Closing Costs.............21

Plan For After-Move-In-Expenses..............23

What Type Of Property To Buy..................24

Research Your Mortgage Options..............25

Compare Mortgage Lenders......................27

Paying Points Isn't A Bad Thing...............29

Get A Prequalified Or Preapproval Letter....30

Hire The Real Estate Agent......................32

Shop Under Your Preapproval Limit.........34

Pick The Right Neighborhood..................35

Go To Open Houses...............................36

Buy A Home For Tomorrow.....................37

Look Past The Little Things.....................39

You Will Have To Compromise.................40

Make A Solid Offer................................41

Avoid A Bidding War.............................42

Negotiate...43

Shopping For Homeowners Insurance........44

Get A Home Inspection..........................46

Closing...48

Foreword

Several months after meeting Wes for the first time, I had the pleasure of getting to work with him one on one. He sought out the coaching program that I co-founded to grow in all areas of his life. I knew from the first call we had together that Wes was an implementer, deeply cared for others, and is a man who gets things done. In the few short months between first meeting Wes in October and us starting to work together in March, Wes and his awesome wife Julie, decided to take control of their lives. They were able to lose of ton weight by sustainable changing the way they lived their lives daily.

I learned 2 things from Wes on that first call. One, that he was ready to make his life better which he had already begun. Two, that he was a man who impacted change that could last, otherwise known as doing it the right way.

As a mortgage industry veteran in the originating, management, and coaching world, I have always stressed quality over quantity. Wes is quality. He will be in this industry long after many others have jumped out, in, and out again. He is exactly the man I want on my team and you should feel fortunate, as you turn the pages of this book, that he is on yours.

Sean Zalmanoff,

Founder, Next Level Loan Officers

Introduction

For a quick introduction, my name is Wesley Wyrick. I am a licensed mortgage lender (NMLS: # 1067576) and I am currently managing a team of lenders in West Virginia. I am licensed in WV, KY, OH, and TN. I have over 18 years of experience in the financial industry and have been fortunate to help hundreds of families with their first home purchase. So trust me when I say that I know that buying a home can be nerve wracking, especially if you're a first-time home buyer. Not only is it probably the biggest purchase of your life, but the process can sometimes be complicated and fraught with unfamiliar lingo and surprise expenses. Over my last 18 years in the financial industry, I have had several conversations with buyers on helping them understand the home buying process. My team and I take pride in trying to help home buyers have an easy and smooth transaction, but sometimes we can run into bumps during the process.

I'd like to try to make the first-time home buying journey a little less stressful for you. With feedback from other lenders and Realtors from across the country, I have compiled these 25 tips to help you navigate the process more smoothly and possibly save some money too.

Tip #1

Start Saving For A Down Payment Early

Now a days, it's not common to put down a 20% down payment like our parents or grandparents did for their first home purchase. Many lenders now permit much less. First-time home buyer programs allow as little as 3% down and in some cases zero down.

Putting down less than 20% could mean higher costs and will more than likely bring PMI

(Private Mortgage Insurance) into the mix. But even a small down payment can still be hefty. For example, a 5% down payment on a $200,000 home is $10,000.

You can play around with a down payment calculator to help get an idea of a comfortable down payment amount. To get the best idea of how much down payment you'll need, it is best to consult with a licensed mortgage lender. Some tips for saving for a down payment include setting aside tax refunds and work bonuses, setting up an automatic savings plan and using an app to track your progress.

Tip #2

How Much House Can You Afford

Before you start looking for your dream home, you'll need to know what's actually within your price range. You can use an online home afford ability calculator to determine how much you can afford, but this isn't going to give you the most accurate reading. Again, I strongly suggest reaching out to a licensed mortgage lender for this part. On the mortgage side, the biggest determining factor in how much house you can afford is your debt to income ratio. The debt to income ratio (DTI) is a calculation on how much money comes in monthly compared to how much money goes out monthly as a percentage.

Example: If your gross monthly income is $5000 and your total monthly liabilities are $2500, your DTI would be 50%.

When calculating DTI, us mortgage lenders, use only credit liabilities along with any legal responsibilities (alimony, child support, etc.). You will also want to include the new mortgage payment including the monthly taxes, insurance, and PMI (Private Mortgage Insurance). Even though it's not calculated in the DTI, you'll also want to consider your other monthly liabilities to make sure that you don't over extend yourself.

Example: child care expenses, cell phone bill, water, electric, gas, car fuel, etc. Even though these expenses aren't calculated in the DTI ratio for your mortgage, you'll want to be aware of how these will affect your monthly budget along with your mortgage and other liabilities. You don't want to over extend yourself.

When calculating the income side, we

look at gross monthly income. Example: If you make $15 per hour and work 40 hours per week, you'll need to calculate it out monthly. $15X40=$600 weekly, $600X52=$31200 annually, $31200/12=$2600 monthly. We can also use additional income like child support, alimony, commissions, bonuses, etc. There are many factors that go into calculating this part. You definitely want to reach out to a licensed mortgage lender for help with this portion.

All loan programs have different DTI maximums. Your lender will be able to review these with you one on one. A typical comfort range is usually around 40% - 45%. But there are programs that will allow up to 56% or even higher.

Tip #3

Understanding Your Credit

When you're taking out a mortgage loan, your credit will not only be one of the key factors in determining whether you're approved or not, but it will also play a role in determining your interest rate and possibly the loan terms. Your credit score is basically your grade on how you handle your debt and pay your bills. The range for a credit score is 300 - 850. Most banks will have their own credit criteria. The government programs that most of us independent lenders have access to, will start in the 500s. But, the higher the score the better the rate and costs.

You will want to check your credit before you begin the home buying process. The only government endorsed site to access your credit report for free is annualcreditreport.com. Here you will have access to all three credit bureaus reports, Experian, Equifax, and TransUnion. You will want to review all three. While looking at your credit, you'll first want to check for any inaccuracies. Under the Fair Credit Act, you have the right to dispute anything that is reporting incorrectly on your credit. Dispute any errors that could be dragging down your credit score. This can take up to 30 to 45 days to complete, so you will want to do this with a sense of urgency. Another way to boost your credit, is to pay down any revolving credit debt below 30% of the available limit. Depending on the lender's requirements, you may also need to address the non-medical collections. You will also want to make sure there isn't any outstanding liens or judgements. The better you understand your credit going into the home financing process, the better it will help you with getting pre-qualified.

Tip #4

Stop Any New Credit Activity

Whenever you open a new credit account, whether it's financing a car or getting a new credit card, the lender runs a hard inquiry, which will ding your credit score. If you're applying for a mortgage soon, avoid opening new credit accounts to keep your score from dropping. Also, after being pre-approved and definitely while under contract to purchase, you absolutely do NOT want to do anything with credit. I have unfortunately seen it happen multiple times. Someone under contract finances their new furniture a few days before closing on their new home and this causes their credit to drop, then new debt hits and kills the deal. They are now the proud owners of new furniture with no home to put it in. Trust me, you don't want to be that person. Avoid making any new purchases or open any new credit accounts until you sign on that dotted line at closing.

Tip #5

Explore Down Payment Options

Are you struggling to come up with enough money for a down payment? Most programs allow you to receive gifted funds for your down payment. So if family wants to pitch in and help, you can receive gifted funds. You will also have to provide documentation of the gift for the lender. Most retirement programs allow you to access your retirement funds for a home purchase. Research your "terms of withdraw" and I recommend you to seek further advice from your financial advisor and/or your accountant before withdrawing funds from a retirement or investment account.

First-time home buyer programs are plentiful,

including federal mortgage programs with Fannie Mae and Freddie Mac that allow loans with only 3% down.

Other low down payment options include:

Federal Housing Administration (FHA) loans, which permit down payments as low as 3.5%.

Veterans Affairs (VA) loans, which sometimes require no down payment at all.

Rural Housing (USDA) loans, which also has a no down payment option.

And some of the in-house bank loan programs will have no down payment options for well qualified borrowers.

Tip #6

Research State And Local Assistance Programs

In addition to federal programs, many states offer assistance programs for first time home buyers with perks such as tax credits, low down payment loans and interest free loans up to a certain amount. You will hear this referred to as DPA programs or down payment assistance programs. All of these programs have different qualifications and requirements. You will have to take a little time to research these. Your county or municipality may also have first-time home buyer programs.

Tip #7

Start Budgeting For Closing Costs

In addition to saving money for a down payment, you'll need to budget for the money required to close your mortgage, which can sometimes be significant. Closing costs generally run between 2% - 5% of your loan amount. You can shop around and compare prices for certain closing expenses, such as homeowners insurance, home inspections, and title searches. You can also ask for the seller to pay for part or even all of your closing costs while negotiating the purchase price. All the loan programs have limits on how much a seller can contribute towards your closing costs and prepaid items. Make sure to review these numbers with you licensed mortgage lender while getting preapproved. You will want to calculate your expected closing costs to help you set your budget.

Tip #8

Plan For After-Move-In Expenses

So closing costs and down payment isn't the only thing you need to save up for before home shopping. Once you've saved for your down payment and budgeted for closing costs, you should also set aside a buffer to pay for move-in or after move-in expenses. This includes paying movers, truck rental, new furnishings, appliances, rugs, updated fixtures, new paint and any other touches you'll want to have when you move in.

Tip #9

What Type Of Property To Buy

You may be interested in buying a single-family home, and that could be ideal if you want a large lot or a lot of room. But if you're willing to sacrifice space for less maintenance and extra amenities, and you don't mind paying a homeowners association fee, a condo or townhome could be a better fit.

Tip #10

Research Your Mortgage Options

Is a 30-year, fixed rate mortgage your best option, or is another loan type right for you? If you can afford larger monthly payments, you can get a lower interest rate with a 20-year or 15-year fixed loan. You can use a mortgage calculator to get an idea if a 15year or 30-year fixed mortgage is a better fit for you. Or you may prefer an adjustable rate mortgage (ARM), which is riskier but guarantees a low interest rate for the first few years of your mortgage. The best way to determine which mortgage option is best for you is by having a conversation with your mortgage lender. If you are buying your forever home and plan to stay there for a while, you'll strongly want to consider going with a fixed rate loan. If you are only to stay in this home temporarily or if it's your "Starter Home" you may want consider an ARM loan. Your mortgage lender can help guide you through this process.

Tip #11

Compare Mortgage Lenders

If you ask me, the most important part of the home financing process is picking the right lender. There are many things you want to consider when making this decision. Before we get into that let me first say... We, mortgage lenders pretty much all do the same thing. We, for the most part, have access to the same products and programs across the board. When choosing the right mortgage lender for your home purchase, you want that decision to be based off of more than just an interest rate. Because, I promise you, if a mortgage lender takes 3 or 4 months to close the same loan that another lender could have closed in 30 days, it wasn't worth saving the few bucks on your monthly payment or a couple hundred dollars in closing costs.

You can get feedback from family and friends on who they have previously used. Make a post on Facebook and see what everyone says. Example: "Hey FB friends... Which mortgage lender do you recommend and why? You can also ask your Realtor for suggestions. Take time to read different lender's reviews. Most will have reviews on Google, Zillow, and Facebook. See what their past clients are saying about them.

Then take time to reach out to the lender. See if they take time to answer your questions, go over your needs, and help you make an educated decision on which program works for you. If they take time to help you with this at the beginning, they will more than likely be there with you every step of the way.

Tip #12

Paying Points Isn't A Bad Thing

Lenders will often allow you to buy discount points, which means prepaying interest upfront to secure a lower interest rate. This is a common thing in a rising rate environment. This is also common when helping a borrower with a less than perfect credit score. In that case, this may be the difference in being approved or denied. There may also be an option for negative points, in which the lender pays some of your closing costs in exchange for a higher interest rate. How long you plan to stay in the house is one of the key factors in determining whether buying points makes sense or not. You'll need to speak to your mortgage lender to help you decide if buying points is worth it for you.

Tip #13

Get Your Prequalified or Preapproval Letter

You can get prequalified, which simply gives you an estimate of how much a lender may be willing to lend based on your income and debts. This is basically equivalent to: Based on what you tell me, I can do this... But as you get closer to buying a home, it's smart to get a preapproval, where the lender thoroughly examines your finances and confirms in writing how much they are willing to lend you and at what terms. This is equivalent to: Based on the documentation that you have provided me, I can do this... Having a preapproval letter in hand makes you look much more serious to a seller and can give you an upper hand over buyers who haven't taken this step.

You definitely want to be at least prequalified before looking at homes. Most Realtors require you to be prequalified or preapproved before looking at homes. Most places won't allow you to write an offer without attaching a prequalification or preapproval letter. Trust me, you don't want to be at a showing of your dream home and not be prequalified or preapproved. Because, the person walking in for the next showing may be looking for the same dream home and may already be preapproved. Who wins in that situation? Make sure you at least get prequalified first.

Tip #14

Hire The Right Real Estate Agent

You'll be working closely with your real estate agent, so you definitely want to find someone you get along with well. The right buyer's agent should be highly skilled, motivated, and knowledgeable about the area. Take time to read their reviews and see what their past clients are saying about them. Ask friends and family for their recommendations. Interview the Realtors that you think you'll get along with. But you will definitely want to work with an agent. Not working with an agent will not help you dodge an expense. You do not pay the Realtors commission. That is paid for by the seller. If a house is listed by a Realtor, it totally makes sense to use a Realtor to represent you and help you negotiate the purchase. They will have your best interest in mind.

Tip #15

Shop Under Your Preapproval Limit

When you are out looking at homes, look for properties that cost a little less than the amount you were approved for. Even though you have a preapproval letter that says that you can afford this much house, it doesn't account for a broken washer or dryer or any other expenses that may arise during homeownership, especially right after you buy. Rather than maxing yourself out, set a lower purchase expectation to leave yourself wiggle room for any possible unexpected expenses.

Tip #16

Pick The Right Neighborhood

Finding the right neighborhood can be just as important as picking the right house. Take some time to research the schools. Even if you don't have kids yet or ever plan to have kids. This is something that still affects a home's value. Look at local safety and crime statistics. How close are the nearest pharmacy, grocery store, hospital, or any other places you'll use regularly? You can also, drive through the neighborhood on different times in the day to check out things like traffic, noise, and activity levels.

Tip #17

Go To Open Houses

You can use this as an opportunity to scope out the neighborhood and your potential neighbors. Most open houses have curious neighbors that like to stop in. During the open house, pay close attention to the home's overall condition, check for any strange smells, look for any stains, or items that are dated or visibly in need of repair. Ask a lot of questions about the home, such as when it was built, when items were last replaced, and ask how old some of the big ticket items are, like HVAC unit, roof, etc. If several other potential buyers are viewing the home at the same time as you, don't hesitate to schedule a second showing or if this house is "the one", you may even go ahead and write that offer. Having a preapproval letter in hand may help.

Tip #18

Buy A Home For Tomorrow

When looking at homes, it's easy to look at properties that meet your current

needs. But when looking at homes, you will also want to consider your future needs. Young newlyweds may want to look at a larger home if they plan to expand their family in the future. Or if you are a couple that have already raised your kids and they have already moved out and started their own families, you may want to consider looking at a smaller or more affordable home for your retirement. Someone may also want to consider future health conditions when selecting a home. Like is this home easy to get in and out of? Or do I really want to walk up and down stairs with a bad knee. Consider your future wants and needs and whether this home will suit them.

Tip #19

Look Past The Little Things

When you're looking at a home, it's easy to get caught up in the small details like paint color, fixtures, and carpets. These are features that are easy and are not very costly to change once the home is yours. It's almost impossible to find the perfect home that has everything you want, so don't let the little details get in the way of your potential dream home.

Tip #20

You Will Have To Compromise

Like I mentioned in tip 19, it's rare to find a house that's perfect in every way. Think carefully about what you're willing to compromise on and what you're not. Example: Anything less than 4 bedrooms and 2 Bathrooms is a deal breaker, but outdated guest bathroom can be tolerated until we can update it later.

Tip #21

Make A Solid Offer

Your offer is something that you should rely on your real estate agent to help you out with. You will want to consider how much under, or even over, the asking price you're willing to pay to obtain your dream home. You definitely don't want to go too low or too high. There is a possibility that there could be multiple offers on the house you writing an offer on. If that is the case, you want to consider tactics that makes your offer more enticing than the others. This is one of those occasions where a preapproval letter could trump a prequalification letter. More than likely, the offer with the preapproval letter will win. Even if it's a slightly lower offer.

Tip #22

Avoid A Bidding War

In a competitive real estate market with very limited inventory, it's very likely you could be bidding on houses that could get multiple offers. When you find a home you love, it's tempting to make a high offer to insure your bid wins. Don't let your emotions take over. Stick to your purchase budget to avoid getting stuck with a mortgage payment that is uncomfortable or that you can't afford.

Tip #23

Negotiate

There are many things that can be up for negotiation in the home buying process, which can result in major savings. Are there any major repairs you can get the seller to cover, either by them fully handling the repairs or by them giving you a credit adjustment at closing? Is the seller willing to pay for any or all of the closing costs? I would say that
9 out of 10 contracts that I get, the seller is covering some of the closing costs. If you're in a buyer's market, you may find that the seller will bargain with you to get the house off the market.

Tip #24

Shopping For Homeowners Insurance

Before you can move forward with closing on your new home, your lender will require you to buy homeowners insurance. You will want to shop around and compare rates to find the best price. Just because you have been with an insurance company for years, doesn't mean that they will give you the best deal for your homeowners insurance coverage. You will also want to look closely at what's covered in the policies. Going with a less expensive policy could mean there are fewer protections and more out-of-pocket expenses if you file a claim. Also know that your insurer can drop your property if it thinks the home's condition isn't up to par. You may have to be prepared to find a new policy quickly if the insurance company sends someone out to look at the property and aren't happy with what they find. You also need to know that flood damage isn't covered by homeowners insurance. If your new home is located in a flood zone, you will be required buy separate flood insurance.

Tip #25

Get A Home Inspection

Once your offer is accepted, you'll want to have a home inspection to examine the property's condition inside and out. This is not the same as an appraisal. This is where an inspector will comb through the property to see if there are any issues with the home. But not all inspections test for things like mold, pests, or structural condition. Be sure to ask the inspector what all they check during the inspection. Make sure the inspector can access every part of the home, such as the roof, attic, and any crawl spaces. Attend the inspection and pay close attention. Don't be afraid to ask your inspector to take a closer look at something. Also, feel free to ask questions. No inspector will answer the question, "Should I buy this house?" You'll have to make this decision after reviewing the reports and seeing what the sellers are willing to fix.

Closing

Thank you for taking time to read through this book. If you have any questions or if you want to get preapproved for you home purchase, feel free to reach out to me. If you would like to get prequalified, visit www.BestMortgageTeam.com or you can connect with me at www.WesleyWyrick.com. Have a blessed day and HAPPY HOUSE HUNTING!!!

Wesley Wyrick

Printed in the USA
CPSIA information can be obtained
at www.ICGtesting.com
LVHW021233261023
762202LV00017B/1263

9 781388 231897